HO

PRACTICAL
FIREARM
SUPPRESSORS

An
Illustrated
Step-by-Step
Guide

KEITH ANDERSON

Desert Publications
El Dorado, AR 71731-1751 U. S. A.

How to Build Practical Firearm Suppressors

by

Keith Anderson

© 1994 by Keith Anderson

Published by Desert Publications
P.O. Box 1751
El Dorado, AR 71731-1751
501-862-2077

ISBN 0-87947-165-4
10 9 8 7 6 5 4 3 2 1
Printed in U. S. A.

Desert Publication is a division of
The DELTA GROUP, Ltd.
Direct all inquiries & orders to the above address.

WARNING

Neither the author nor the publisher assumes any responsibility for the use or misuse of the information contained in this book. The author and publisher specifically disclaim any personal liability, loss, or risk incurred as a consequence of the use and application, either directly or indirectly, of any advice or information presented herein.

This publication is designed to provide accurate and authoritative information in regard to the subject matter covered. It is sold with the understanding that the author or the publisher are not engaged in rendering professional service. If expert assistance is required, the services of a competent professional person should be sought.

Be advised that there may be certain items represented in this book as to which the sale, possession, construction or interstate transportation thereof may be restricted, prohibited or subject to special licensing requirements. Consult with your local ATF and law enforcement authorities in your area before obtaining or constructing such items.

Technical data and safety procedures presented herein, inevitably reflects the author's individual beliefs and experience with particular equipment and environments under specific circumstances which the reader cannot duplicate or experience exactly. The information in this book should therefore be used for guidance only and should be approached with great caution.

Since neither the author nor the publisher have control over the materials used, use of techniques or equipment, or the abilities of the reader, no responsibility, either implied or expressed, is assumed for the use or misuse of the data or procedures given in this book.

FOR INFORMATION PURPOSES ONLY

TABLE OF CONTENTS

INTRODUCTION

This book is written for people who have more than a passing interest in silencers, as well as those who just want something cheap and easy to build.

While most of the suppressors in this book are designed to be cheap and very simple to build, they are also intended to provide a good degree of service and long lasting performance. The legal applications of silencers are numerous. Varmint hunters not wishing to scare the rest of the game away can find them valuable. Survivalist and para-military groups have numerous uses for them, as do collectors and enthusiasts who simply enjoy silent shooting.

Many people who have experimented with home-made silencers know how it feels to spend a lot of time building one and taking it to the range, and then having it work for only one or two shots. Or, even worse, blow right off the gun on the first shot. The suppressors in this book are designed with these problems in mind, with the intention of keeping them to a minimum.

It should be understood, by anyone who wishes to build a firearm suppressor, exactly how they work and what their limitations are. The bulk of the noise is created by the rapidly expanding gases coming from the barrel. This is the noise that is acted upon by the suppressor. In a nutshell, a suppressor is a chamber, or series of chambers, which is designed to contain the expanding gases while allowing the bullet to pass through.

The second cause of firearm noise is the supersonic crack made by the bullet as it breaks the sound barrier. This one is unfortunately more difficult to deal with. However, this noise alone is very difficult to locate by hearing, so depending on your needs you may not need to worry about it. If it is a concern, however, you can choose a caliber which travels slower than 1100 feet per second, which is the speed of sound. Or use subsonic ammo, which is specifically designed to travel slower than sound. This ammo is available from specialty suppliers in most calibers, including .22 Long Rifle.

The third source of sound is the noise created by the action of the gun. This is especially true of semi-automatic weapons. Normally, this sound is drowned out by the muzzle blast, but when the muzzle is suppressed it becomes more audible. This noise is very small compared to the other sounds created, and as long as they are effectively suppressed, it will not be a great problem. A solution would be to, for example, choose a bolt action rifle instead of a semi-auto. But, even with a bolt action, you have noise created by the action when you cycle the bolt.

It is not recommended that you work with revolvers. Revolvers have a gap between the cylinder and barrel which allows gases to escape, creating a substantial amount of noise. No matter how well you suppress the noise at the front of the barrel, this problem will always exist.

The suppressor designs in this book are effective and very simple to build. They are also very adaptable. This means that they can be built to almost any size, and one way or another, fitted to almost any firearm with an exposed barrel on the front. They can also be built using different construction methods, from cheap, disposable types to good quality, more permanent types. This depends upon the user and his needs. It requires only a little ingenuity to build a good suppressor to suit any special requirements.

All the materials for constructing these units are readily available in any hardware or home improvement store, mostly in the plumbing section. Only a few basic tools are required for the simpler models, such as a drill, hacksaw, and flathead screwdriver. The two higher quality models shown require a wire-feed arc welder, a grinder and a drill press. The welder can be rented, and a machine shop can do the drilling if you don't have the large bits required.

The reader should be aware that the law prescribes severe penalties for assembling or possessing silencers without the proper licenses. Anyone not wishing to risk these consequences should contact their local BATF office about obtaining the proper licenses before starting any construction.

PART ONE
.22 Rimfires

RUBBER CAP SUPPRESSOR #1

This suppressor works by utilizing multiple expansion chambers. This is achieved by constructing the unit with several rubber plumbing test caps placed in succession. These caps are available in the plumbing section of any hardware or home improvement store.

As the bullet passes through the caps, each one acts as a separate expansion chamber, containing more and more of the gases successively. Since the bullet passes through so many rubber baffles, there is no need to replace them with every few shots. This unit is effective until the whole thing comes apart at the seams, and that will take several hundred rounds if it is built properly.

This suppressor is only effective with .22 caliber firearms. This particular one is designed to screw on to the threaded barrel of a TEC-22 pistol.

Materials for construction, (Fig. 1)

One roll each; $1\frac{1}{2}$" or 2" wide strapping tape, 2" black duct tape, $\frac{3}{4}$" masking or strapping tape, black electrical tape.

One roll of gauze or some other light fabric; 1 bolt, $\frac{1}{2}$" with SAE threads, any length; 1 galvanized coupling, $\frac{3}{8}$" to $\frac{1}{2}$"; 1 galvanized or brass pipe nipple, $\frac{1}{2}$" x 2"; 1 piece of PVC pipe, 2" wide by 2" long; 4 rubber plumbing test caps, 2" size.

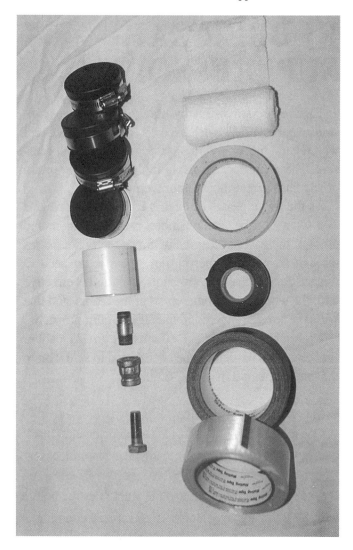

Step 1, (Fig. 2)

Take the bolt and the galvanized coupling. Using wrenches, force the bolt to thread into the small end of the coupling in order to cross-thread it. Work it in and out a few times to make the new threads smooth. The bolt has the same threading as the barrel of the pistol, so with this done, the coupling will now thread onto the barrel.

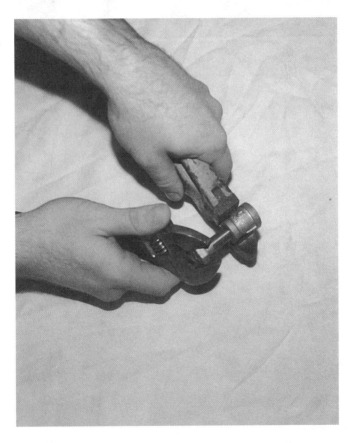

Step 2, (Fig. 3)

Take the pipe nipple and screw it tightly into the large end of the coupling.

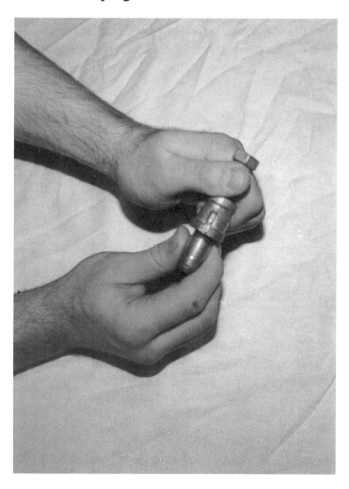

Step 3, (Figs. 4,5)

Use tape to build up the coupling and nipple to the same round diameter. Use masking tape on the nipple end, and electrical tape on the coupling end, because electrical tape is more flexible and the coupling is irregular.

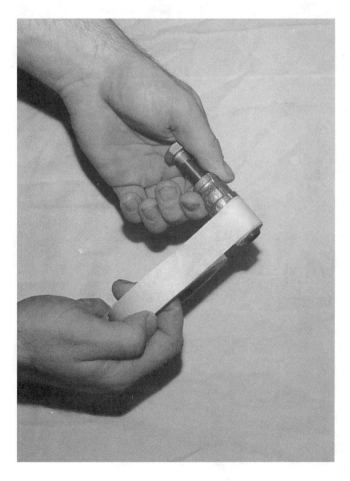

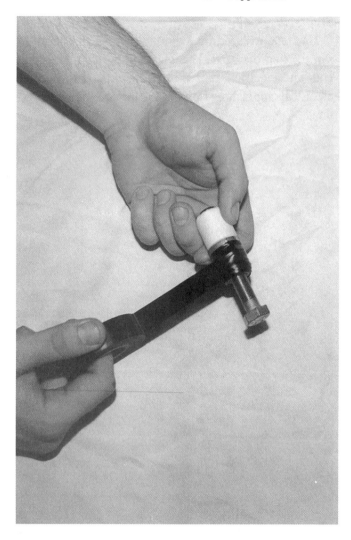

Step 4, (Figs. 6,7)

Use the duct tape to build up the whole thing to where it will just fit tightly into the PVC pipe. Cut the tape and slide the pipe onto the front of the tape buildup, leaving about ¾" of space in the front.

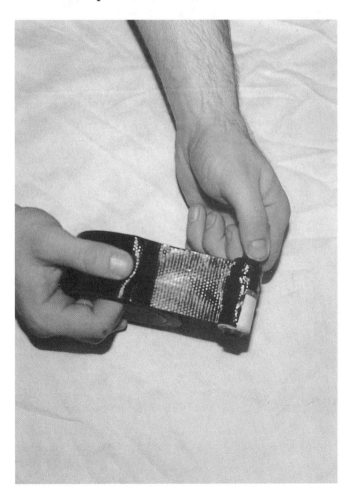

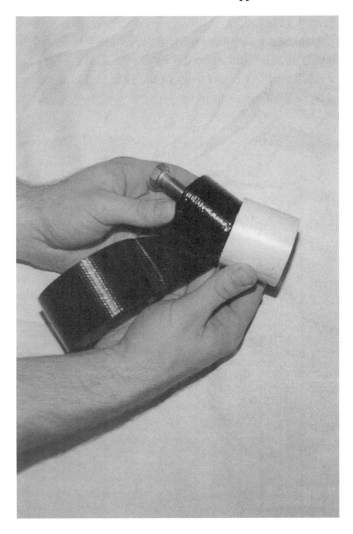

Step 5, (Fig. 8)

Place one rubber cap onto the front of the PVC pipe. Tighten the clamp, but not so tightly as to distort the shape of the cap.

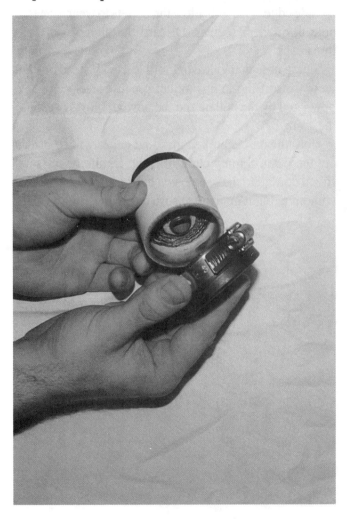

Step 6, (Fig. 9)

Pack the other three caps loosely with gauze. Do it by folding it into squares as shown, then packing it in with a thinner layer in the center and the bulk of it around the outside edge. This will allow the bullets to wear a cleaner hole through the center. Discard the clamps on these three caps.

Please note that gauze or cloth is used instead of steel wool for stuffing in this model because steel wool gets powdered by the bullets and the powder blows back into the gun.

Until the unit is broken in, some gauze will be blown out the front. Simply cut it off with a knife or scissors. If you don't like the gauze, you can build the suppressor without it, but it may not absorb the sound quite as well.

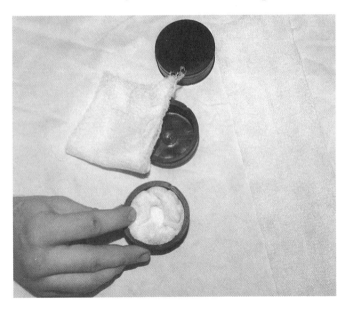

Step 7, (Figs. 10,11)

Place the three caps onto the front of the first one. Secure them in place by wrapping a few loops of wide strapping tape completely around both ends. Keep the caps on straight as you do so. Then wrap a few loops around both ends across the other sides so that all sides are covered. Then, starting at the front, wrap the outside in strapping tape from front to back. Make it several layers thick for strength.

Step 8, (Figs. 12,13)

Wrap the unit with black duct tape in the same way for additional strength and appearance. Wrap a few loops around both ends, covering all sides, then wrap around the outside from front to back.

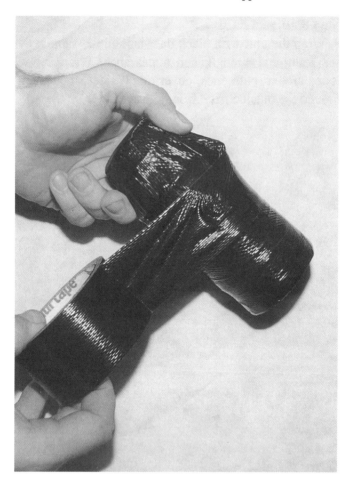

Step 9, (Fig. 14)

Using a sharp knife, cut out a hole in the tape where the barrel threads into the coupling. Thread the unit onto the pistol.

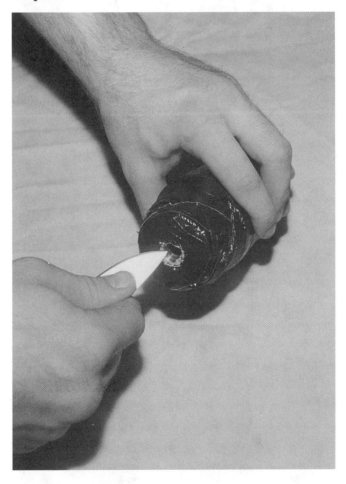

(Fig. 15)
   Completed unit attached to TEC-22 pistol.

EXPANSION CHAMBER SUPPRESSOR

This unit is designed to suppress while maintaining a higher level of accuracy. While rubber cap silencers work well with pistols at close range, the deflection is too great to make them suitable for rifle shooting at any distance. The following suppressor uses a larger, longer expansion chamber with only a single cap. Which reduces the need for all the rubber baffles, because there is more volume to contain the gases. This unit is designed to fit on the flash suppressor of a Ruger 10/22.

Materials for construction, (Fig. 1)
One piece of 2" PVC pipe, 12" long; one 2" rubber test cap; $1\frac{3}{4}$" hose clamp; 1 piece of gray threaded PVC pipe, $\frac{3}{4}$" by 12" long; 1 roll of $\frac{3}{4}$" strapping tape; 1 roll of 2" black duct tape; 1 package of coarse steel wool.

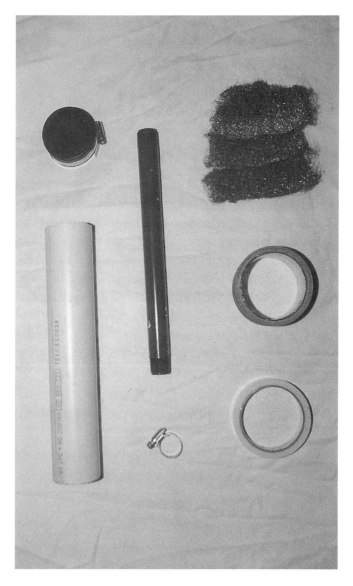

Step 1, (Fig. 2)

Take the piece of gray PVC. The inside of one end of this pipe is slightly larger than the inside of the other end. The larger end is the right size to fit over the flash suppressor. Take a hacksaw and cut two slits in the end, crossways from each other, to facilitate clamping. Make them about 1" deep.

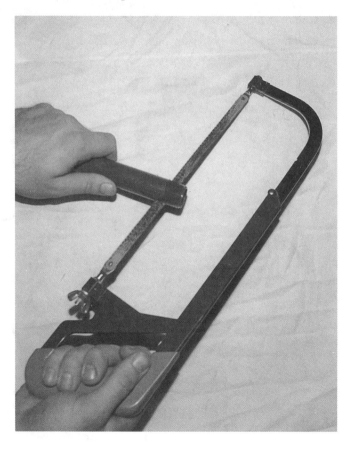

Step 2, (Fig. 3)

Drill vent holes down the length of the pipe. Start them 1" from the slits on the back end and finish 1" from the front end. Use a $\frac{1}{4}$" bit, and space the holes about 1" apart. Cover all sides of the pipe. Don't drill so many as to weaken the pipe though.

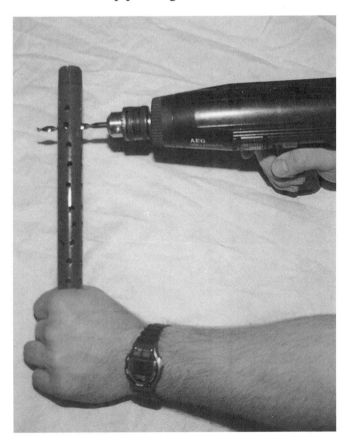

Step 3, (Figs. 4,5)

Use the strapping tape to build up the walls on the ends of the gray pipe. On the end with the slits, make it an inch from the end so as not to cover the slits. On the front end, make it right on the end. Build up the walls to where the 2" PVC pipe will just fit snugly over them.

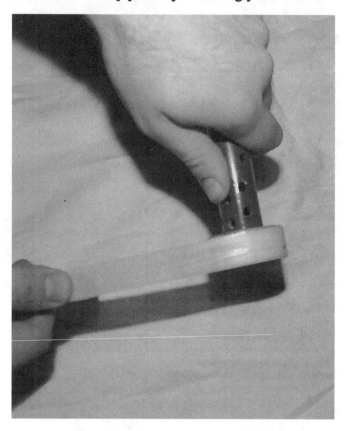

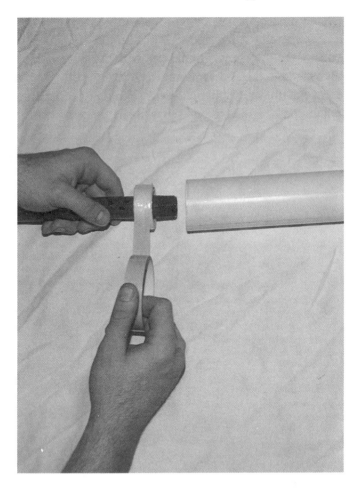

Step 4, (Fig. 6)

Starting with the front end first, slide the gray pipe down the inside of the 2" pipe, while packing the 2" pipe with steel wool as you go. Stop sliding it in when the back tape wall is even with the end of the 2" pipe. This will leave a 1" space in the front end.

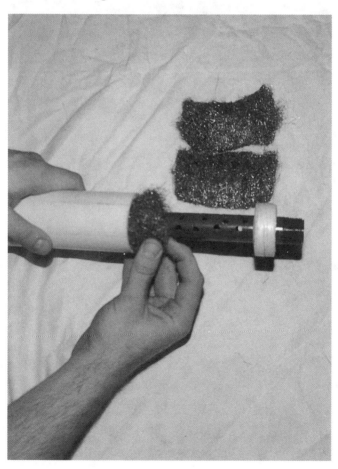

Step 5, (Fig. 7)

Place about 10 strips of strapping tape over the back end of the 2" pipe. Make them about 8" long. This will prevent the 2" pipe from sliding forward off the rest of the unit when the gun is discharged.

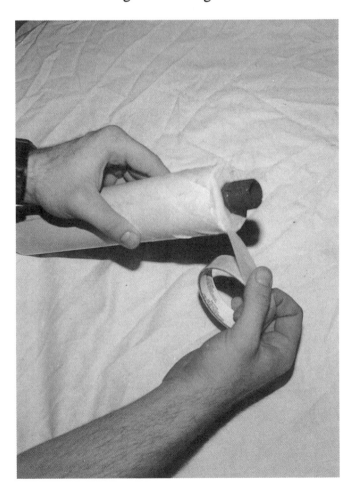

Step 6, (Fig. 8)

Wrap the length of the 2" pipe with black duct tape for appearance and to hold the strapping tape on the back in place.

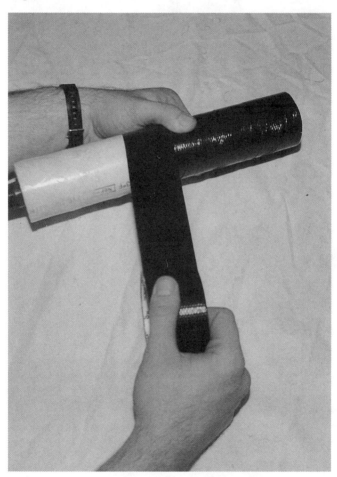

Step 7, (Fig. 9)

Place the rubber cap on the front end of the unit and tighten the clamp.

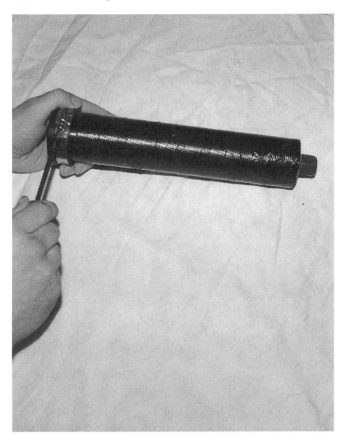

Step 8, (Fig. 10)

Place the small hose clamp on the end of the gray PVC pipe where the slits are located. Slide the end of the gray pipe onto the flash suppressor and tighten the clamp. Picture shows completed unit attached to a Ruger 10/22.

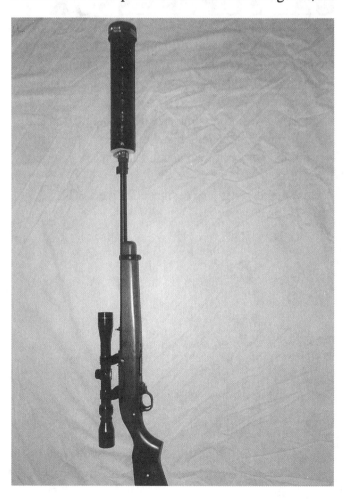

EXPANSION CHAMBER/RUBBER CAP SUPPRESSOR

The following is one example of how expansion chambers can be combined with a series of rubber caps to create a "hybrid" suppressor which can be custom designed for your own specific needs according to accuracy, level of suppression, size of the suppressor, and so on. By varying the length and diameter of the chamber, and the number of caps, you can achieve a variety of results.

This suppressor is also designed for the TEC-22.

(Fig. 1)

Shown is the expansion chamber with the extra caps. The chamber has been constructed by first, re-threading the galvanized coupling as described in the *Rubber Cap Suppressor #1* section, then screwing a 6" length of ½" metal pipe into the large end. Metal pipe is used instead of PVC for pistols because the greater concussion from a pistol barrel will break up or melt a plastic pipe. Then the vent holes are drilled in the pipe and the rest of the expansion chamber is constructed around it as described in the *Expansion Chamber Suppressor* section. The chamber shown is 6" long by 2" wide, with one 2" rubber cap already clamped on the end.

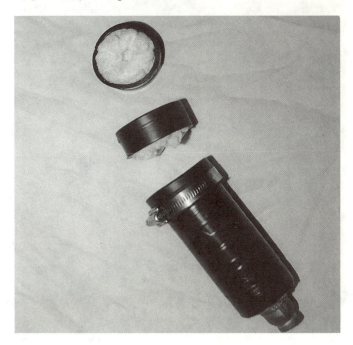

(Fig. 2)

The additional caps, already packed with gauze, are placed on top of the first cap and secured with wide strapping tape. Several strips of the tape about 10" long are placed over the front of the caps and down the sides of the chamber. It is not necessary to wrap the tape completely around the back end. Place the strips of tape so that all sides of the caps and chamber are covered. Then, starting at the front, wrap strapping tape around the outside of the caps and down onto the outside of the chamber. Make this outside wrapping several layers thick.

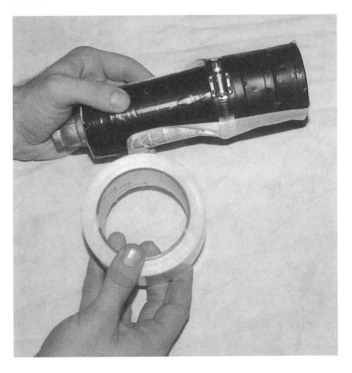

(Figs. 3,4)

Repeat the taping procedure with black duct tape for appearance and additional strength. Start by placing a few strips over the front and down the sides, covering all sides. Then wrap the outside with a few layers, covering all the strapping tape.

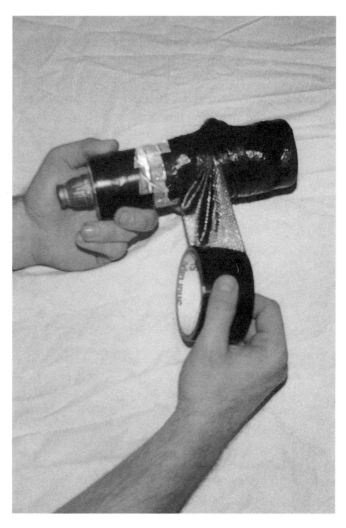

(Fig. 5)
Completed unit attached to TEC-22 pistol.

This design can be experimented with and altered to suit your needs. For example, longer and/or wider expansion chambers will absorb more of the gases. More caps will contain more of the gases effectively. Fewer caps will result in better accuracy, because of the decreased deflection.

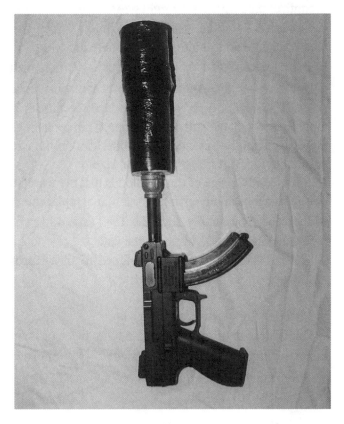

RUBBER CAP SUPPRESSOR #2

This unit is a more advanced, better quality version of the first Rubber Cap suppressor. It is a solid metal welded unit which is intended to last a lifetime, requiring only a periodic replacement of the rubber caps. It utilizes a length of pipe which is the right size so that $1\frac{1}{2}$" rubber caps will fit down the inside of it. While a 2" cap will clamp on the end to hold them in. There are two good sources for this type of pipe. One is $2\frac{3}{8}$" thin wall galvanized conduit. Another is $2\frac{3}{8}$" chain link fence poles. The second type is recommended, because it is more lightweight but still plenty strong. The size listings may vary slightly. Just try a 2" rubber cap on the end before buying. If it fits, it's the right size.

Another advantage of this method is that there are no messy tape jobs involved in construction or replacement of the caps. You simply slide the $1\frac{1}{2}$" caps down the pipe and clamp one 2" cap onto the end.

The unit presented here is designed to fit a Ruger Mark II pistol with a standard barrel.

Materials for construction (Fig. 1)

One 5" length of outer pipe; one scrap piece of sheet metal, $\frac{1}{8}$" thick; one piece of $\frac{1}{2}$" conduit, $1\frac{3}{4}$" long; one 1" hose clamp; five $1\frac{1}{2}$" rubber caps and one 2" cap.

Step 1, (Fig. 2)

Cut a very short piece of the outer pipe to use as a tracing ring. Use a marker to trace the inside of the ring onto the sheet metal.

Step 2, (Fig. 3)

Cut out the general shape around the circle. Stay at least $\frac{1}{8}$" outside the circle.

Step 3, (Fig. 4)

Grind the circle down to the outside diameter of the outer pipe. Place it on the end to check the fit.

Step 4, (Fig. 5)

Find the center of the circle. Use a center punch to mark it for drilling.

Step 5, (Figs. 6,7)

Using a small drill bit, drill a pilot hole in the center of the endplate. Enlarge the hole until the $\frac{1}{2}$" conduit just fits through.

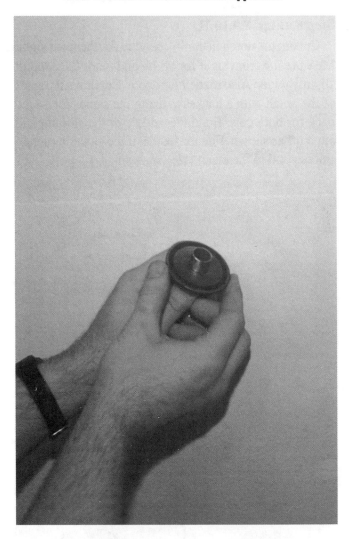

Step 6, (Figs. 8,9,10,11)

Cut out the notch in the ½" conduit for the front sight. Measure the front sight for width and mark the conduit slightly wider. Also mark it for depth. Cut down the sides of the notch with a hacksaw, using the same slot on the back for both cuts. Bend the middle of the slot out and cut it off as shown. File the inside of the slot completely smooth and to the exact size you want.

Step 7, (Fig. 12)

Place the piece of conduit into the endplate hole. Use a wire-feed welder to tack just the bottom side in place.

Step 8, (Fig. 13)

Place the endplate onto the end of the outer pipe and weld it into place. You may want to remove the galvanizing from the parts to be welded, because breathing the fumes can make you ill.

Step 9, (Fig. 14)

Use tape to cover the barrel in order to protect it from scratching and make a tighter fit for clamping.

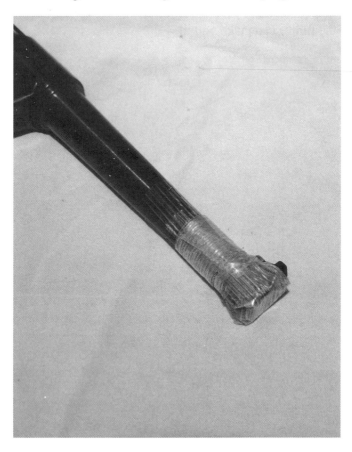

Step 10, (Fig. 15)

Clamp the unit onto the barrel and insert a cleaning rod into the barrel. Use this as a gauge to adjust the unit so that the outer pipe is well centered.

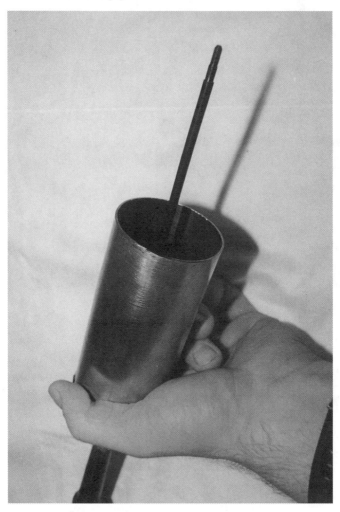

Step 11, (Fig. 16)

Remove the unit from the barrel and complete the weld around the center. Grind off the excess metal from both the welds.

Step 12, (Fig. 17)

Paint the unit, if desired. Black auto primer provides a good, non-reflective coating.

Step 13, (Fig. 18)

Insert the small rubber caps into the outer tube, and clamp the 2" cap onto the end.

(Fig. 19)

Completed unit attached to Ruger Mark II pistol.

This suppressor can be made longer or shorter if you desire. The 1½" caps are about 1" wide, so just make the outer pipe the same number of inches long as the number of caps you want to put inside.

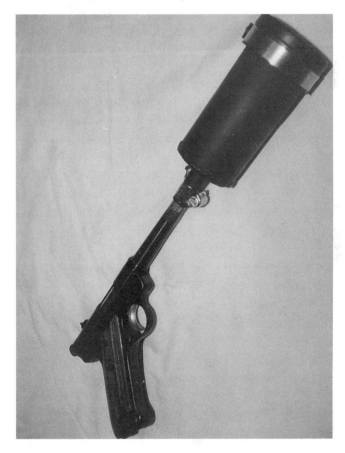

PART TWO
Large Calibers

If you are a beginner at constructing gun suppressors, it is recommended that you start by working with .22 rimfires before attempting to build one for a large caliber weapon.

Larger guns are more powerful and dangerous, and the suppressors require stronger and more careful construction in order for them not to blow apart. Other than that, the principles involved in making them are exactly the same; with the exception that they need to be larger to contain the amount of gases the guns produce.

This section contains two examples of effective methods for building large caliber suppressors. One is for an oversize 9mm pistol, the other is a sniper rifle-type suppressor for an AR-15. While they may seem a bit large, (and they are), that is unfortunately what you must deal with if you want them to work over extended periods of shooting. You can make them smaller if you want, but don't plan on them working for more than about three shots before the caps need to be replaced.

9MM SUPPRESSOR

This unit is designed for a Calico 9mm pistol.

Materials for construction, (Fig. 1)

One piece of $\frac{1}{2}$" conduit, 12" long; 1 piece of 2" PVC, 10" long; 1 roll each: 2" wide black duct tape, $1\frac{1}{2}$" or 2" strapping tape, $\frac{3}{4}$" strapping tape; 1 package of coarse steel wool; five 2" rubber test caps; 1 package of flathead wood screws, size $\frac{3}{4}$ x 6; two $\frac{3}{4}$" hose clamps.

Step 1, (Fig. 2)

Take the ½" conduit and drill the vent holes. Start drilling the holes 1" from the front end and stop about 3" from the back end. File all the burrs smooth.

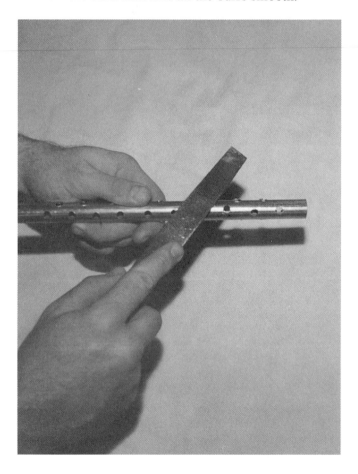

Step 2, (Fig. 3)

Use the ¾" strapping tape to build up the tape walls as described previously. They must be wrapped tightly for strength, and must fit inside the 2" PVC very snugly. Make the front wall right on the front end, and the back one 2" from the back end of the conduit.

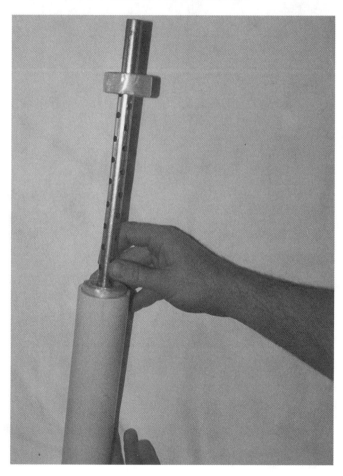

Step 3, (Fig. 4)

Cut two slits crossways on the back end of the conduit for clamping. Make them about $1\frac{1}{2}$" deep.

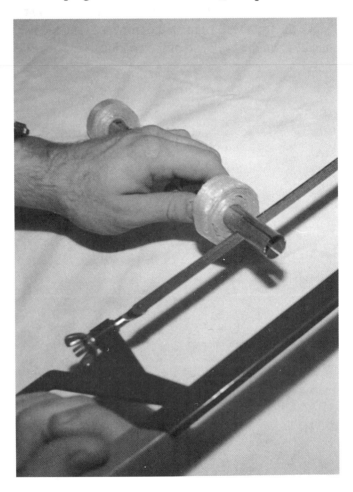

Step 4, (Fig. 5)

Slide the center pipe down inside the outer pipe, stuffing it with steel wool as you go. Stop when the tape walls are even with the ends of the outer tube.

Step 5, (Fig. 6)

Using a $\frac{1}{8}$" bit, drill four holes in each end of the outer pipe directly over the tape walls. Do not drill into the tape walls.

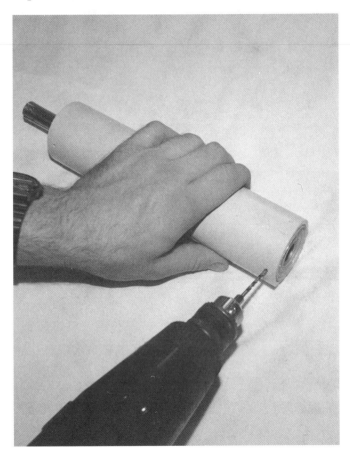

Step 6, (Fig. 7)

Using a $\frac{3}{8}$" bit, countersink the holes for the screw heads.

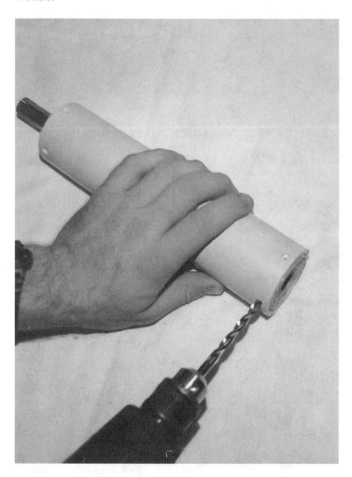

Step 7, (Fig. 8)

Thread the screws through the holes and into the tape walls. Tighten them down flush with the outer tube.

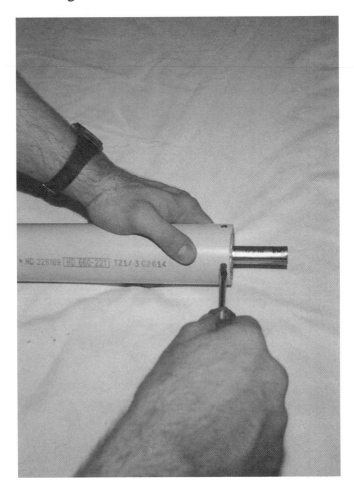

Step 8, (Fig. 9)

Wrap the outer tube in black duct tape.

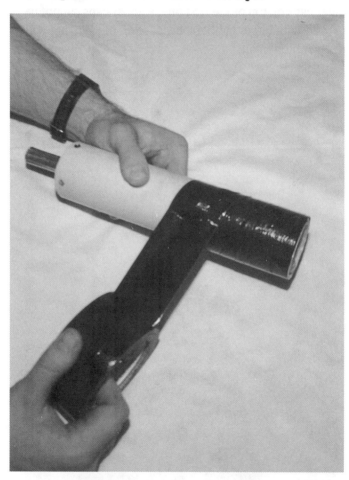

Step 9, (Fig. 10)

Clamp one cap onto the end of the unit and place the other caps on top of the first one. Rubber caps cannot be packed with larger calibers, because all the stuffing will just get blown out.

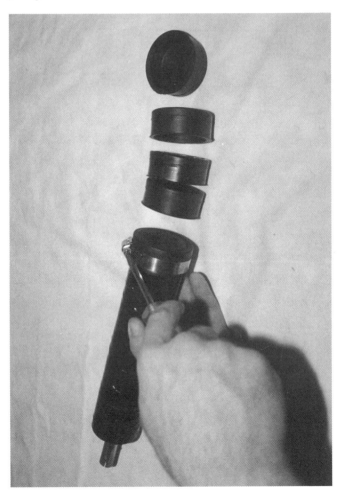

Step 10, (Fig. 11)

Place at least ten strips of wide strapping tape over the end of the unit as shown to hold the caps in place. Cover all sides.

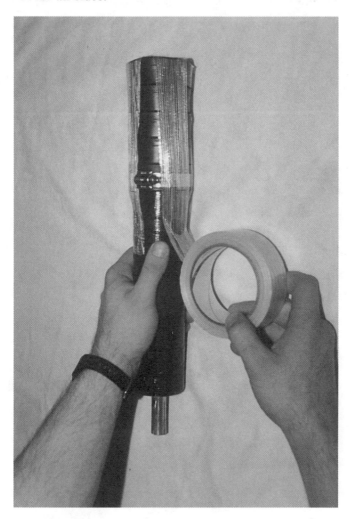

Step 11, (Fig. 12)

Wrap around the outside of the unit from front to back as shown. Make this wrapping several layers thick for strength.

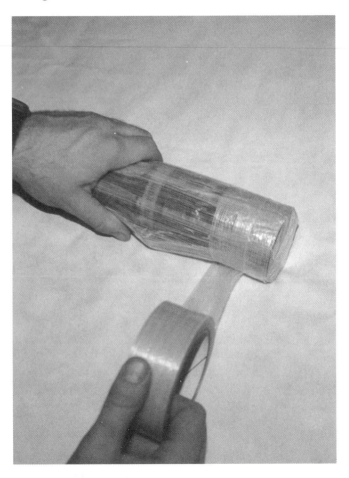

Step 12, (Fig. 13)

Cover all the strapping tape with black duct tape for appearance.

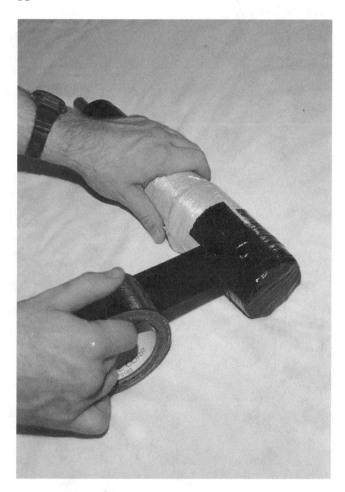

Step 13, (Fig. 14)

Put a couple layers of tape over the barrel of the gun to protect it from being scratched. Then clamp the unit onto the barrel.

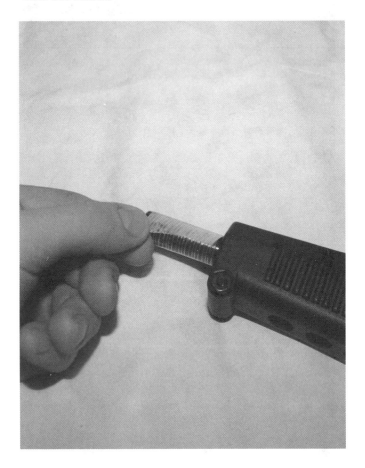

(Fig. 15)

Completed unit attached to Calico 9mm pistol. Two clamps are used to help keep it straighter.

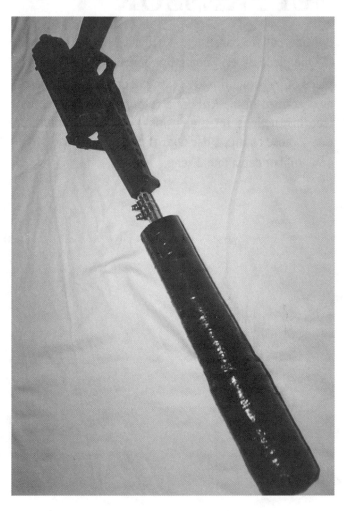

.223 (5.56mm) SUPPRESSOR

Materials for construction, (Fig. 1)

One piece of 2⅜" chain link fence pole, 24" long; 1 piece of ¾" conduit, 20¼" long; 2 endplates, prepared as described in the *Rubber Cap Suppressor #2* section (see instructions for dimensions); 1 flash suppressor; one 1" hose clamp; 1 package of coarse steel wool; four 1½" rubber caps; one 2" cap.

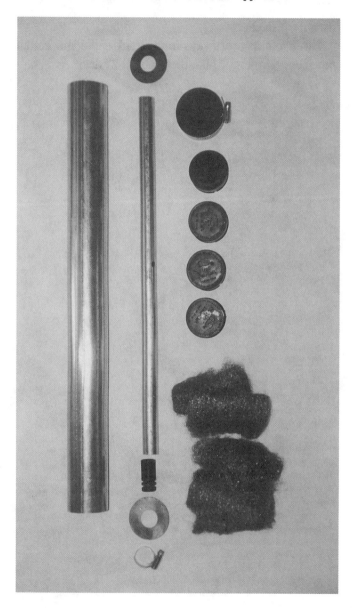

Step 1, (Fig. 2)

Cut two slits crossways in the back end of the center pipe for clamping. Make them about 2" deep.

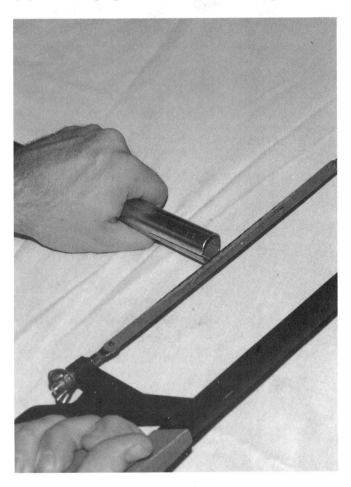

Step 2, (Fig. 3)

Insert the flash suppressor into the center tube and clamp it solidly into place as shown.

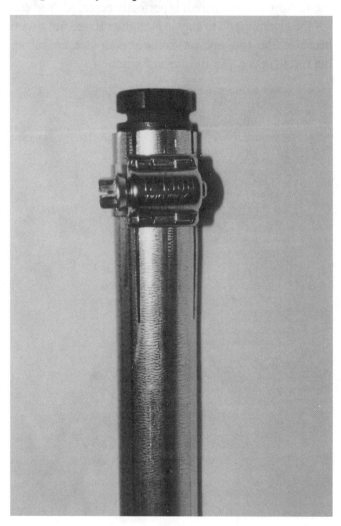

Step 3, (Fig. 4)

Thread the flash suppressor and center tube onto the rifle barrel, and use a cleaning rod to check the alignment. Adjust it to where it is perfectly centered. You can get the cleaning rod to stay in straighter if you put a wire brush on the end, and put some scotch tape farther up the rod to make it fit the barrel tighter.

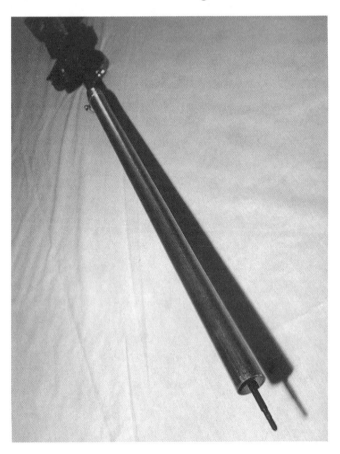

Step 4, (Fig. 5)

Remove the flash suppressor and center tube from the gun and weld them securely together with a wire-feed welder. Start by welding just the very end of the tube. Then remove the hose clamp and weld the slits closed. Be careful not to burn through the conduit. Once the welding is complete, grind off the excess metal so that the back endplate will slide over the end. Then thread it back onto the rifle barrel to make sure the tube is still centered.

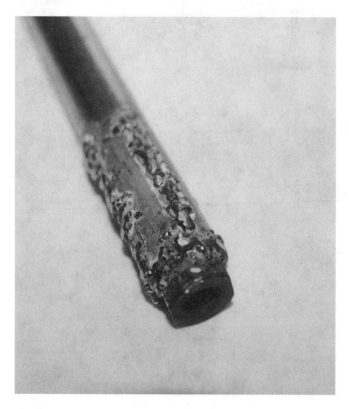

Step 5, (Fig. 6)

Drill the vent holes and weld the front endplate onto the front end of the tube. Start the vent holes one inch from the front end, and stop one inch from the welded slits on back. The endplate has been drilled to the same diameter as the center tube, (in this case $15/16$"), and the outer diameter is the same as the inside diameter of the outer tube. This is so it can slide down inside.

Step 6, (Fig. 7)

Slide the front endplate and center tube down the outer tube, stuffing it with steel wool as you go. Leave $\frac{1}{4}$" of the center tube sticking out the end.

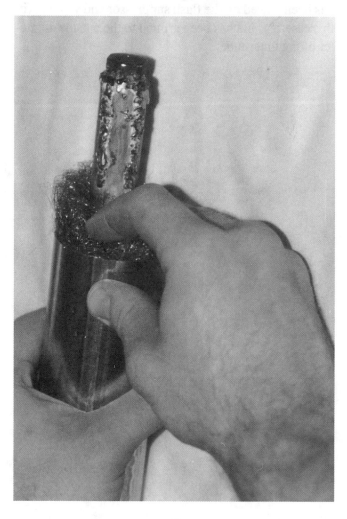

Step 7, (Fig. 8)

Place the back endplate over the end of the center tube and firmly against the outer tube. This endplate has been drilled slightly larger to fit over the center tube after it has been placed on the flash suppressor and welded, (in this case 1"), and has been ground to the outside diameter of the outer tube.

Step 8, (Fig. 9)

Weld the endplate onto the outer tube first, then weld the center tube in place. Grind off the excess metal. If you're a good enough welder, you can weld the front endplate to the inside of the outer tube. Be careful, because that plate is four inches down inside and you can't get a grinder down there to fix your mistakes. If you don't weld it, it will hold up fine anyhow.

Step 9, (Fig. 10)

Paint the unit, if desired.

Step 10, (Fig. 11)

This design will leave four inches of space in the front end. Slide the 1½" caps down inside and clamp the 2" cap on the end. This method of clamping the end cap will only withstand subsonic ammo. In order to use full power ammo, a stronger capping method is required. Following are two examples of how this can be accomplished.

Capping method #1, (Fig. 12)

This photo is pretty self-explanatory. A black 2" ABS cap has been placed on the end of the unit in place of the 2" rubber cap. ABS plumbing parts are similar to PVC, but are much stronger. A 1" hole has been drilled in the center of the cap. The cap has been secured with four $\frac{1}{2}$ x 14 sheet metal screws. The screw hole size is $\frac{13}{64}$". Also, a $\frac{1}{2}$" hole has been drilled through the center of every rubber cap inside. This is necessary to prevent the bullets from being deflected into the ABS cap. Drilling holes through the caps will also restore the weapon's accuracy if you have been careful to keep everything centered during construction.

Capping method #2, (Fig. 13,14,15)

This is a stronger way to cap the suppressor, and will withstand more firing than previous methods. With this method, four $1\frac{1}{2}$" ABS caps are used in place of the four rubber caps. First a $\frac{1}{2}$" holes is drilled in the exact center of each cap. Then the caps are placed down the end of the suppressor. Holding the last cap down securely, side holes are drilled through the suppressor and into the sides of the front cap. The screw hole size is $\frac{13}{64}$". Once the holes are drilled, the front cap is secured in place with $\frac{1}{2}$ x 14 sheet metal screws.

Both methods shown here will suppress full power .223 ammo down to about the level of a .22 rimfire rifle. The first method will withstand about 20 rounds before the noise level begins to slowly increase. The second method will withstand approximately 100 rounds, if they are not fired too quickly. To use either method, it is essential that the center tube, as well as the entire unit, be centered. This can be determined by firing the unit with just one 2" rubber cap on the end of the unit, and checking where the exit hole is made. It should be right on center.

(Fig. 16)

Completed unit attached to a Colt AR-15.

CONCLUSION

By now you should be able to see how much potential for variations there are in these designs. The rubber test caps used are available in sizes from $1\frac{1}{2}$" up to 4", which means that some very large or very small expansion chambers can be made if you desire.

Because subsonic ammo is so important for silent shooting, we are including the address of a company from which it can be ordered. The address is:

Phoenix Systems
PO Box 3339, Evergreen, CO 80439

Their catalog costs $2.00. Subsonic ammo is also available in many pistol calibers from some gun stores or law enforcement supply stores.

When using subsonic ammo, you can usually get by with smaller suppressors. Modifications to the recoil spring may be necessary for this ammo to cycle properly, because it is not as powerful as full charged ammo. This will depend upon the caliber used and the gun.

Please exercise appropriate caution when using suppressors. Personal risk is small; however, using a suppressor can increase the amount of pressure inside a gun. Only firearms in good condition should be used. If you use the same gun with a suppressor often, you should have it checked by a gunsmith regularly for damage or excessive wear and tear.

If the suppressor isn't built or attached to the gun strongly enough, it can blow apart. Even then, it will usually just blow off from the front of the gun harmlessly. Bystanders should stand to the rear of the shooter, just in case of flying debris. Shooting glasses are also not a bad idea.

Something else you should be aware of is that the increased pressure can affect the operation of the gun. In other words, it can cause the gun to jam more frequently. Better quality firearms seem to be less prone to this problem. For example, the author's tests showed that the Ruger Mark II didn't jam at all, while the TEC-22 jammed fairly consistently. You may want to consider this when selecting a gun.

With a little care and common sense, suppressed firearm shooting can be a successful and enjoyable hobby, or more serious venture. Good luck!

WORKS CONSULTED

from:
Desert Publications
P.O. Box 1751
El Dorado, AR 71730-1751 U. S. A.
1-800-852-4445

NOTES

NOTES

NOTES

How To Build Practical Firearm Suppressors

NOTES

NOTES

NOTES

Other Books Available From Desert Publications

No.	Title	Price
001	Firearms Silencers Volume 1	$9.95
003	The Silencer Cookbook	$9.95
004	Select Fire Uzi Modification Manual	$9.95
005	Expedient Hand Grenades	$16.95
007	007 Travel Kit, The	$8.00
008	Law Enforcement Guide to Firearms Silencer	$8.95
009	Springfield Rifle, The	$11.95
010	Full Auto Vol 3 MAC-10 Mod Manual	$9.95
012	Fighting Garand, The	$11.95
013	M1 Carbine Owners Manual	$9.95
014	Ruger Carbine Cookbook	$11.95
015	M-14 Rifle, The	$9.95
016	AR-15, M16 and M16A1 5.56mm Rifles	$11.95
017	Shotguns	$11.95
019	AR15 A2/M16A2 Assault Rifle	$8.95
022	Full Auto Vol 7 Bingham AK-22	$9.95
027	Full Auto Vol 4 Thompson SMG	$9.95
030	STANAG Mil-Talk	$12.95
031	Thompson Submachine Guns	$12.95
033	H&R Reising Submachine Gun Manual	$12.95
035	How to Build Silencers	$6.95
036	Full Auto Vol 2 Uzi Mod Manual	$9.95
049	Firearms Silencers Vol 3	$13.95
050	Firearm Silencers Vol 2	$9.95
054	Company Officers HB of Ger. Army	$11.95
056	German Infantry Weapons Vol 1	$14.95
058	Survival Armory	$27.95
060	Survival Gunsmithing	$9.95
061	FullAuto Vol 1 Ar-15 Mod Manual	$8.95
064	HK Assault Rifle Systems	$27.95
065	SKS Type of Carbines, The	$16.95
066	Private Weaponeer, The	$9.95
067	Rough Riders, The	$24.95
068	Lasers & Night Vision Devices	$29.95
069	Ruger P-85 Family of Handguns	$9.95
071	Dirty Fighting	$11.95
072	Live to Spend It	$29.95
073	Military Ground Rappelling Techniques	$11.95
074	Smith & Wesson Autos	$27.95
080	German MG-34 Machinegun Manual	$9.95
081	Crossbows/ From 35 Years With the Weapon	$11.95
082	Op. Man. 7.62mm M24 Sniper Weapon	$7.95
083	USMC AR-15/M-16 A2 Manual	$16.95
084	Urban Combat	$21.95
085	Caching Techniques of U.S. Army Special Forces	$9.95
086	US Marine Corps Essential Subjects	$16.95
087	The L'il M-1, The 30 Cal. M-1 Carbine	$14.95
088	Concealed Carry Made Easy	$9.95
089	Apocalypse Tomorrow	$7.95
090	M14 and M14A1Rifles and Rifle Marksmanship	$16.95
091	Crossbow As a Modern Weapon	$11.95
092	MP40 Medicine	$11.95
093	Map Reading and Land Navigation	$11.95
094	U.S. Marine Corps Scout/Sniper Training Manual	$16.95
095	Clear Your Record & Own a Gun	$14.95
096	Sig Handguns	$16.95
097	Poor Man's Nuclear Bomb	$19.95
098	Poor Man's Sniper Rifle	$19.95
100	Submachine Gun Designers Handbook	$16.95
101	Lock Picking Simplified	$8.50
102	Combination Lock Principles	$8.50
103	How to Fit Keys by Impressioning	$7.95
104	Keys To Understanding Tubular Locks	$9.95
105	Techniques of Safe & Vault Manipulation	$9.95
106	Lockout - Techniques of Forced Entr	$11.95
107	Bugs Electronic Surveillance	$9.95
110	Improvised Weapons of Amer. Undergrnd	$10.00
111	Training Handbook of the American Underground	$10.00
114	FullAuto Vol 8 M14A1 & Mini 14	$9.95
116	Handbook Bomb Threat/Search Procedures	$9.95
117	Improvised Lock Picks	$10.00
119	Fitting Keys By Reading Locks	$7.00
120	How to Open Handcuffs Without Keys	$9.95
121	Electronic Locks Volume 1	$9.95
122	With British Snipers...To the Reich	$24.95
125	Browning Hi-Power Pistols	$9.95
126	P-08 Parabellum Luger Auto Pistol	$9.95
127	Walther P-38 Pistol Manual	$9.95
128	Colt .45 Auto Pistol	$9.95
129	Beretta - 9MM M9	$11.95
130	FullAuto Vol 5 M1 Carbine to M2	$9.95
132	Ranger Handbook	$16.95
133	FN-FAL Auto Rifles	$13.95
135	AK-47 Assault Rifle	$11.95
136	Uzi Submachine Gun	$9.95
137	USMC Battle Skills Training Manual	$24.95
140	Sten Submachine Gun, The	$9.95
141	Terrorist Explosives Handbook	$6.95
142	U.S. Army Counterterrorism Training Manual	$14.95
143	Sniper Training	$24.95
144	The Butane Lighter Handgrenade	$8.95
146	The Official Makarov Pistol Manual	$17.95
152	Glock's Handguns	$17.95
154	Heckler and Koch's Handguns	$17.95
156	The Poor Man's Ray Gun	$9.95
200	Fighting Back on the Job	$11.95
202	Secret Codes & Ciphers	$14.95
204	Improvised Munitions Black Book Vol 1	$14.95
205	Improvised Munitions Black Book Vol 2	$14.95
206	CIA Field Exp Preparation of Black Powder	$8.95
207	CIA Field Exp. Meth/Explo. Preparat	$8.95
209	CIA Improvised Sabotage Devices	$12.00
210	CIA Field Exp. Incendiary Manual	$12.00
211	Science of Revolutionary Warfare	$9.95
212	Agents HB of Black Bag Ops.	$9.95
214	Electronic Harassment	$11.95
217	Improvised Rocket Motors	$6.95
218	Impro. Munitions/Ammonium Nitrate	$8.95
219	Improvised Batteries/Det. Devices	$5.95
221	Impro. Explo/Use In Deton. Devices	$7.95
222	Evaluation of Imp Shaped Charges	$8.95
225	American Tools of Intrigue	$12.00
255	Impro. Munitions Black Book Vol 3	$25.00
226	Poor Man's James Bond Vol 2	$24.95
227	Explosives and Propellants	$11.95
229	Select Fire 10/22	$11.95
230	Poor Man's James Bond Vol 1	$24.95
231	Assorted Nasties	$9.95
234	L.A.W. Rocket System	$8.00
240	Clandestine Ops Man/Central America	$11.95
241	Mercenary Operations Manual	$9.95
250	Improvised Shaped Charges	$8.95
251	Two Component High Exp. Mixtures	$8.95
260	Survival Evasion & Escape	$13.95
262	Infantry Scouting, Patrol, & Sniping	$13.95
263	Engineer Explosives of WWI	$7.95
300	Brown's Alcohol Motor Fuel Cookbook	$13.95
301	How to Build a Junkyard Still	$11.95
303	Alcohol Distillers Handbook	$17.95
306	Brown's Book of Carburetors	$11.95
310	MAC-10 Cookbook	$9.95
350	Cheating At Cards	$12.00
367	Brown's Lawsuit Cookbook	$18.95
400	Hand to Hand Combat	$7.95
401	USMC Hand to Hand Combat	$7.95
402	US Marine Bayonet Training	$8.95
404	Camouflage	$12.95
409	Guide to Germ Warfare	$13.95
410	Emergency War Surgery	$24.95
411	Homeopathic First Aid	$9.95
412	Defensive Shotgun	$12.95
414	Hand to Hand Combat by D'Eliscue	$7.95
415	999 Survived	$6.00
416	Sun, Sand & Survival	$6.00
420	USMC Sniping	$16.95
424	Prisons Bloody Iron	$13.95
425	Napoleon's Maxims of War	$6.95
429	Invisible Weapons/Modern Ninja	$11.95
432	Cold Weather Survival	$11.95
435	Homestead Carpentry	$10.00
436	Construction Secret Hiding Places	$9.95
437	US Army Survival	$29.95
438	Survival Shooting for Women	$11.95
440	Survival Medicine	$11.95
442	Can You Survive	$9.95
443	Canteen Cup Cookery	$5.95
444	Leadership Hanbook of Small Unit Ops	$11.95
445	Vigilante Handbook	$11.95
447	Shootout II	$14.95
448	Catalog of Military Suppliers	$8.95
454	Survival Childbirth	$8.95
455	Police Karate	$10.95
456	Survival Guns	$21.95
457	Water Survival Training	$5.95
470	Emergency Medical Care/Disaster	$11.95
500	Guerilla Warfare	$14.95
504	Ranger Training & Operations	$14.95
508	Spec. Forces Demolitions Trng HB	$9.95
508	IRA Handbook	$9.95
510	Battlefield Analysis/Inf. Weapons	$9.95
511	US Army Bayonet Training	$7.95
512	Desert Storm Weap. Recog. Guide	$7.95
542	Professional Homemade Cher Bomb	$10.95
544	Combat Loads for Sniper Rifles	$12.00
551	Take My Gun..If You Dare	$10.95
552	Aunt Bessie's Wood Stove Cookbook	$7.50
605	Jackedup & Ripped off	$10.00
C-002	Trapping & Destruc. of Exec. Cars	$10.00
C-011	How To Open A Swiss Bank Account	$6.95
C-020	Defending Your Retreat	$9.95
C-021	How To Become A Class 3 MG Dealer	$6.95
C-021	Methods of Long Term Storage	$3.95
C-023	How To Obtain Gun Dealer Licenses	$3.95
C-025	Confid. Gun Dealers Guide/Whlesler	$2.50
C-028	Federal Firearms Laws	$5.00
C-029	Militarizing the Mini-14	$6.95
C-030	M1 Carbine Arsenal History	$6.95
C-030	OSS/CIA Assassination Device	$4.00
C-038	Hw To Build A Beer Can Morter	$11.95
C-040	Criminal Use of False ID	$11.95
C-050	Surviving Doomsday	$11.95
C-052	CIA Explosives for Sabotage	$9.00
C-058	Brass Knuckle Bible	$7.95
C-080	USA Urban Survival Arsenal	$7.95
C-085	Dead or Alive	$7.95
C-099	Elementary Field Interrogation	$9.95
C-175	Beat the Box	$7.95
C-177	Boobytraps	$9.95
C-209	Guide/Vietcong Boobytraps/Device	$8.00
C-386	Self-Defense Requires No Apology	$11.95
C-679	M16A1 Rifle Manual Cartoon Version	$6.95
C-9031	Become a Licensed Gun Collector	$4.95
FP-9	Micro Uzi Select Fire Mod Manual	$9.95

PRICES SUBJECT TO CHANGE WITHOUT NOTICE

Send $5.00 for a complete 72 page catalog Free with order

DESERT Publications
P.O. Box 1751 Dept. BK-165
El Dorado, AR 71730-1751 USA

Add $5.95 to all orders for shipping & handling.